Copyright © 2021 by Hallie Bradley
All rights reserved. This book or any portion there of may not be reproduced or used in any manner whatsoever without the express written permission of the publisher except for the use of brief quotations in a book review.

ISBN: 978-1-7347562-1-0

THE SCAVENGER HUNT COLORING BOOK

This book is prepared for educational fun. Use this coloring book with your children or students to learn new vocabulary and then take it with you to see if students can use the new vocabulary they've learned and find everything.

The scavenger hunt lists in this book can be used in a variety of ways. If you're not going to the seaside, use The Seaside List as you read a storybook about the beach. Use The Insect List when you head to a science museum. No matter where you live, you can use these lists to add a fun activity into your weekend routine or homeschooling lesson. Don't have a farm near you? Go over the vocabulary and have your kids color in the shapes. Then, have them make their own story about a farm in which they must use each animal on the list. As they use the animals and farm equipment in the story, they can mark it off of their scavenger hunt list. Think outside of the box and these scavenger hunt lists can go along with numerous activities whether you're outside, traveling, or just staying at home.

The Lists In This Book

- My Nature List
- My Body Part List
- My Transportation List
- My Insect List
- My Farm List
- My Sea Creature List
- My Hotel List
- My Fall List
- My Winter List
- My Spring List
- My Summer List
- My Market List
- My Moon Phase List
- My Seaside List
- My Art Class List
- My Musical Instrument List
- My Mammal List
- My Bird List
- My Reptile & Amphibian List
- My Fish List
- My Dinosaur List
- My Shape List
- My Airport List
- My Forest List

MY NATURE LIST

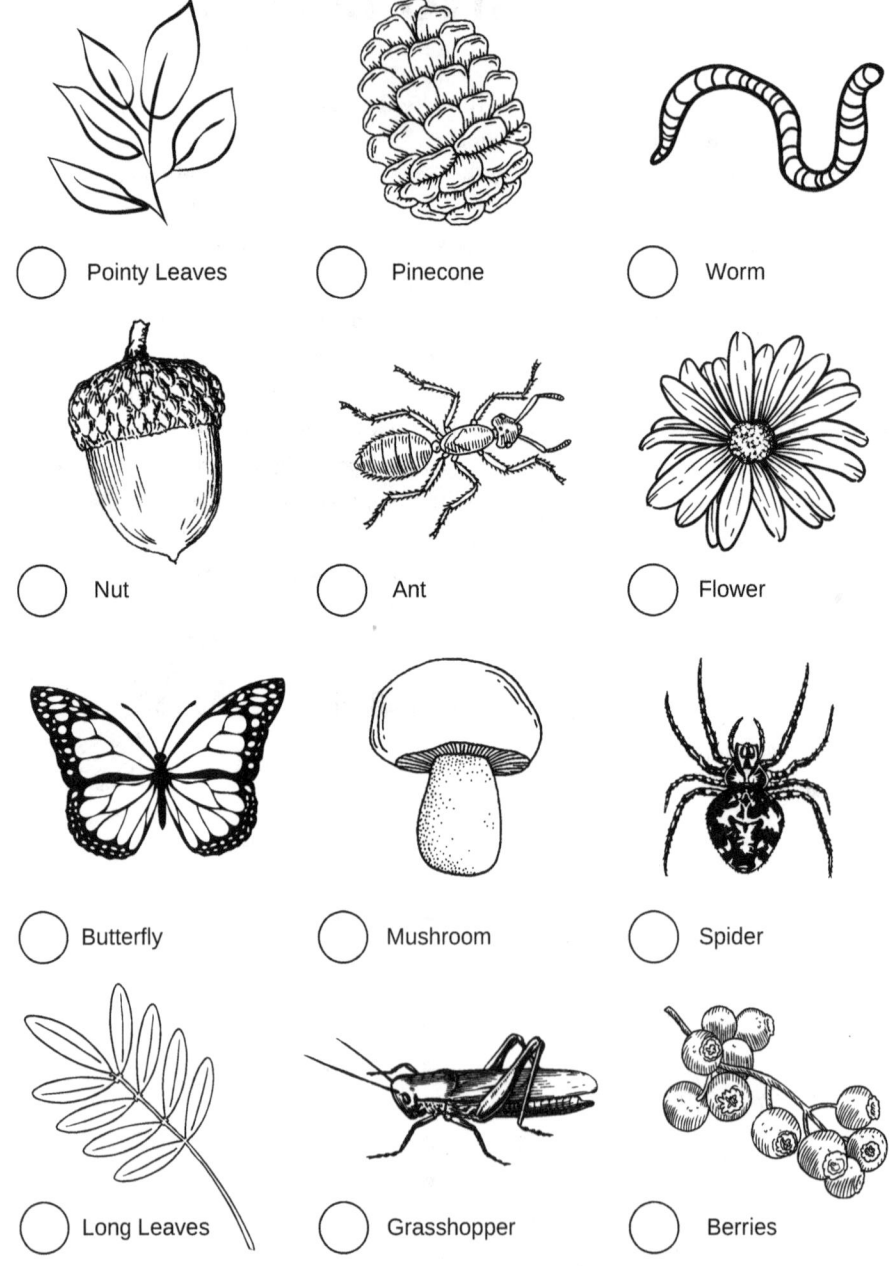

MY NATURE LIST

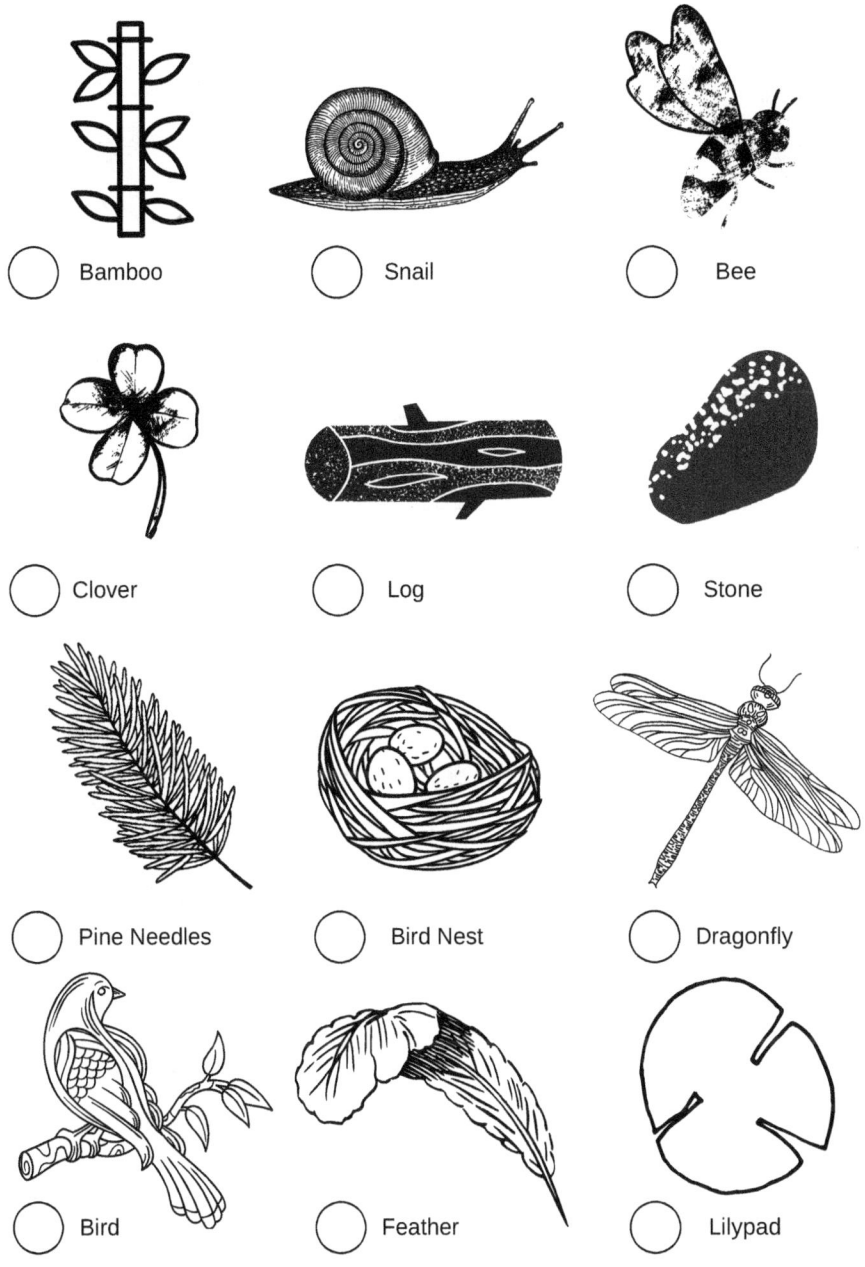

○ Bamboo   ○ Snail   ○ Bee

○ Clover   ○ Log   ○ Stone

○ Pine Needles   ○ Bird Nest   ○ Dragonfly

○ Bird   ○ Feather   ○ Lilypad

MY BODY PART LIST

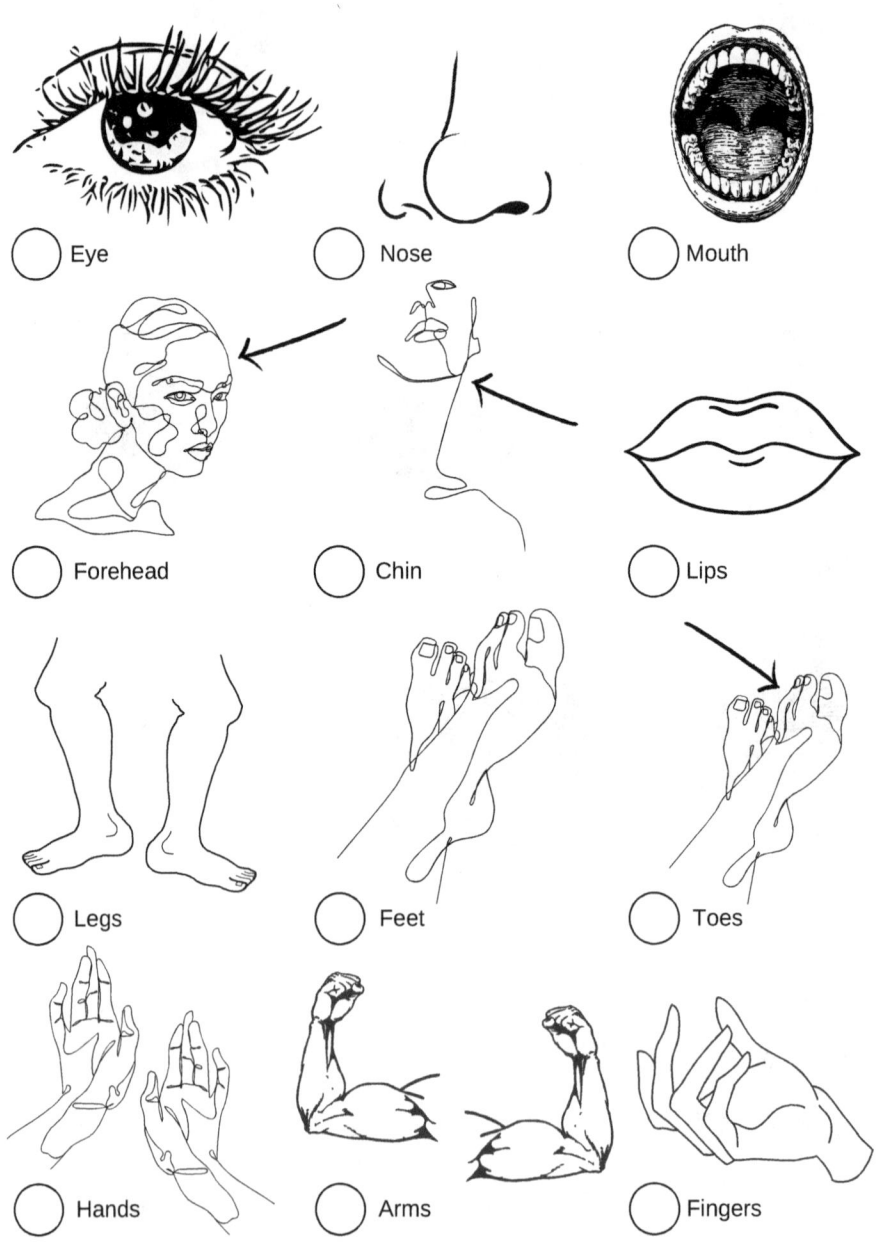

MY BODY PART LIST

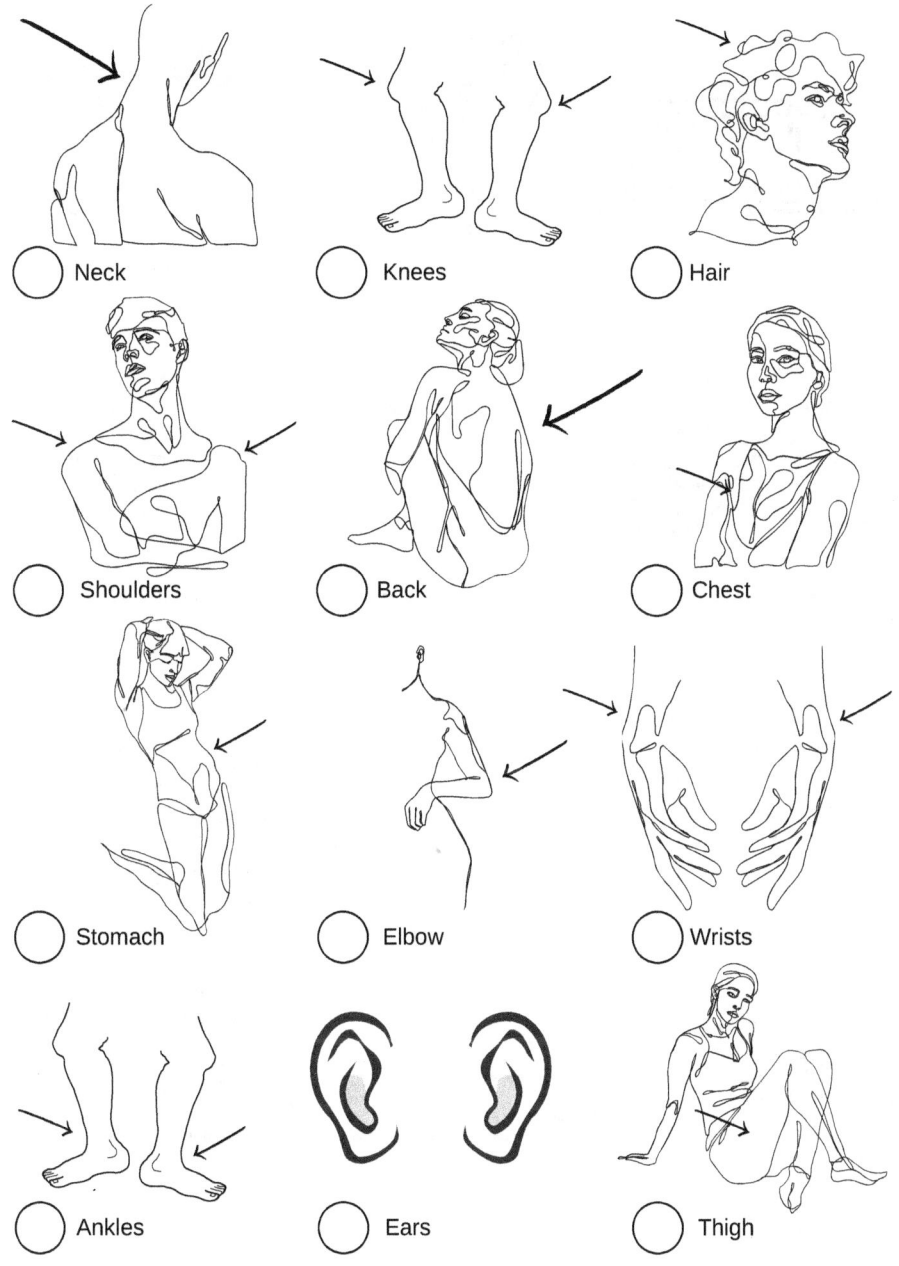

MY TRANSPORTATION LIST

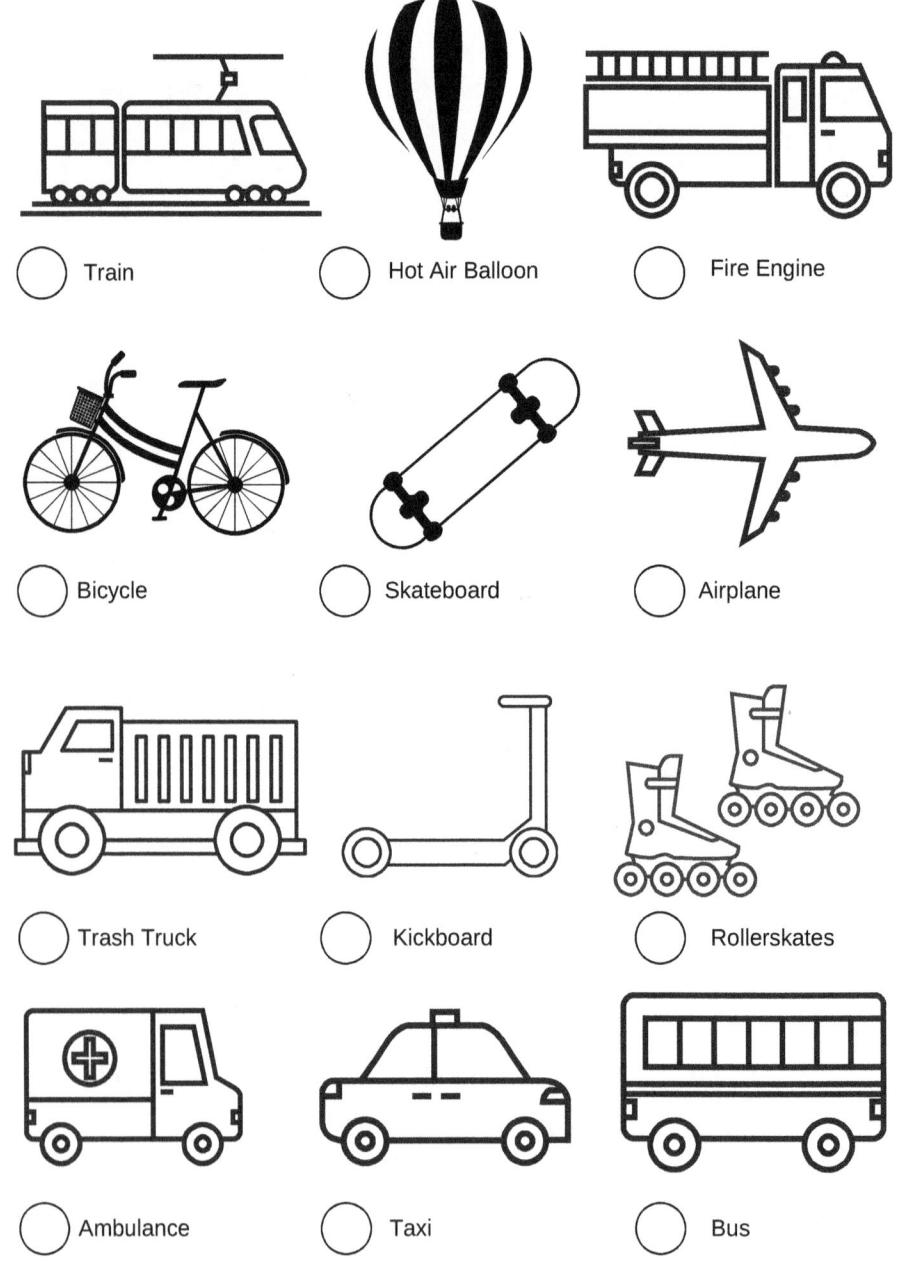

MY TRANSPORTATION LIST

- ◯ Cement Truck
- ◯ Cable Car
- ◯ Dump Truck
- ◯ Car
- ◯ Truck
- ◯ Ice Skates
- ◯ Boat
- ◯ Double Decker Bus
- ◯ Sail Boat
- ◯ Motorcycle
- ◯ Food Truck
- ◯ Fork Lift

MY INSECT LIST

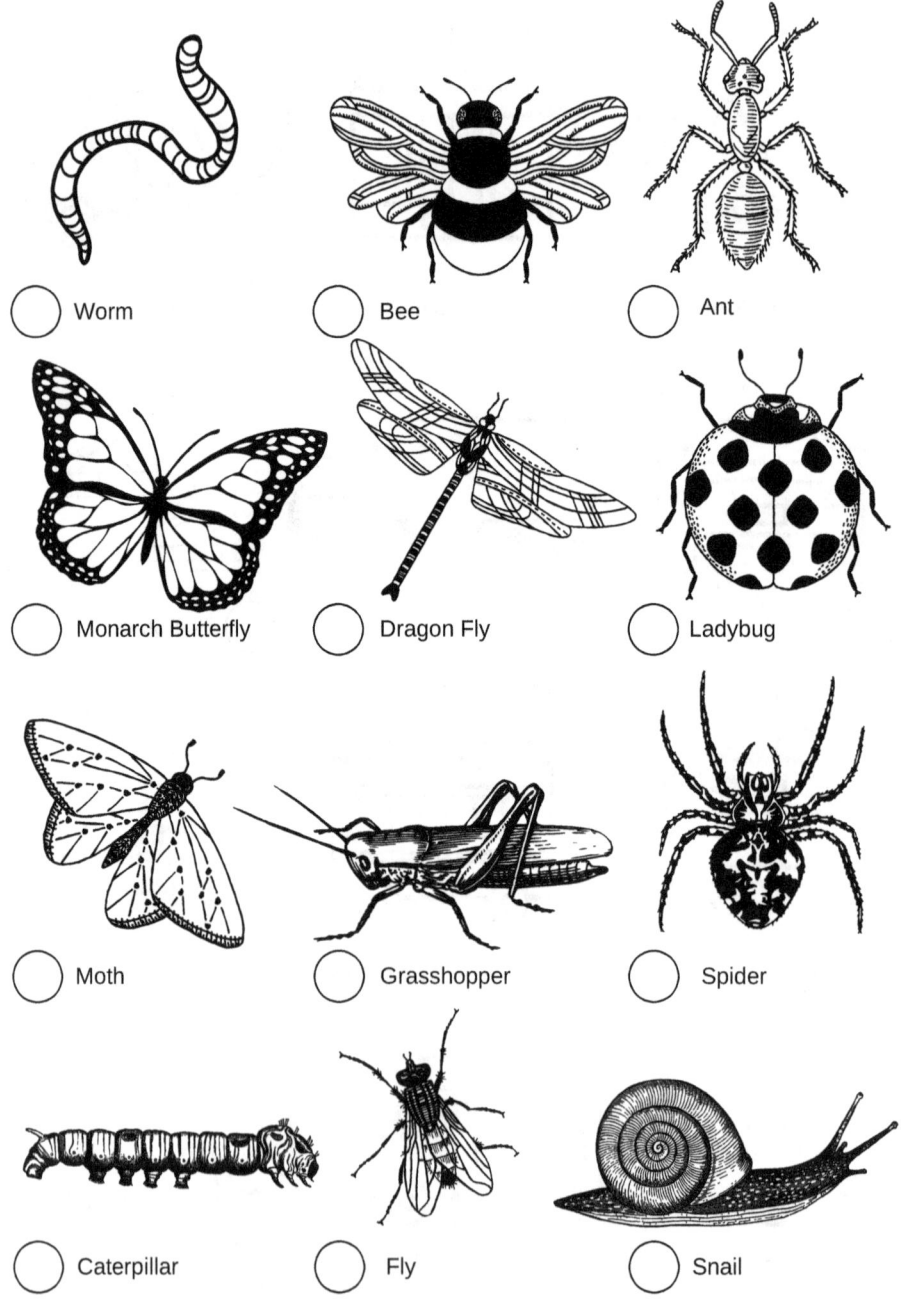

- ○ Worm
- ○ Bee
- ○ Ant
- ○ Monarch Butterfly
- ○ Dragon Fly
- ○ Ladybug
- ○ Moth
- ○ Grasshopper
- ○ Spider
- ○ Caterpillar
- ○ Fly
- ○ Snail

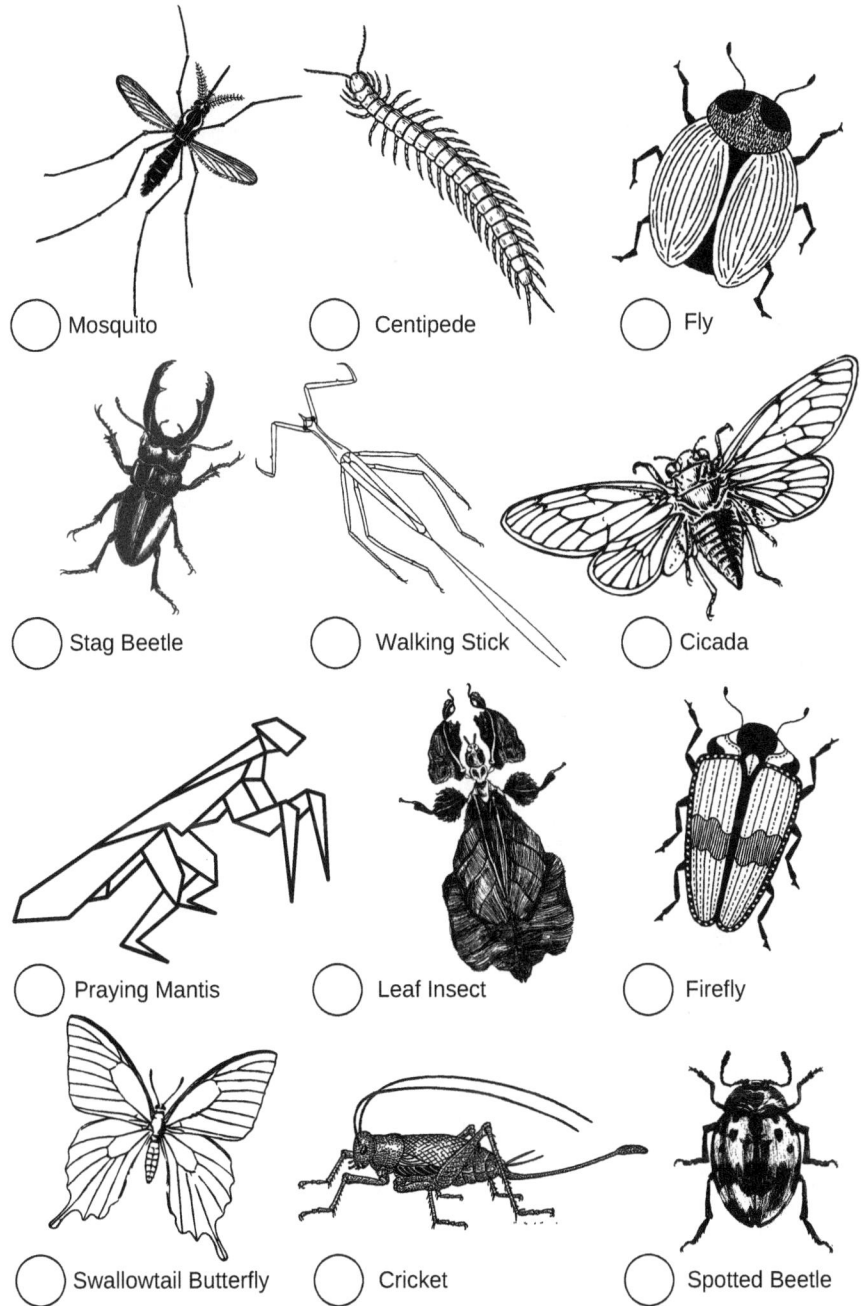

MY FARM LIST

MY FARM LIST

○ Fence ○ Eggs ○ Farmer

○ Barn ○ Bucket ○ Hen

○ Sheep ○ Chicks ○ Goat

○ Apples ○ Corn ○ Carrots

MY SEA CREATURE LIST

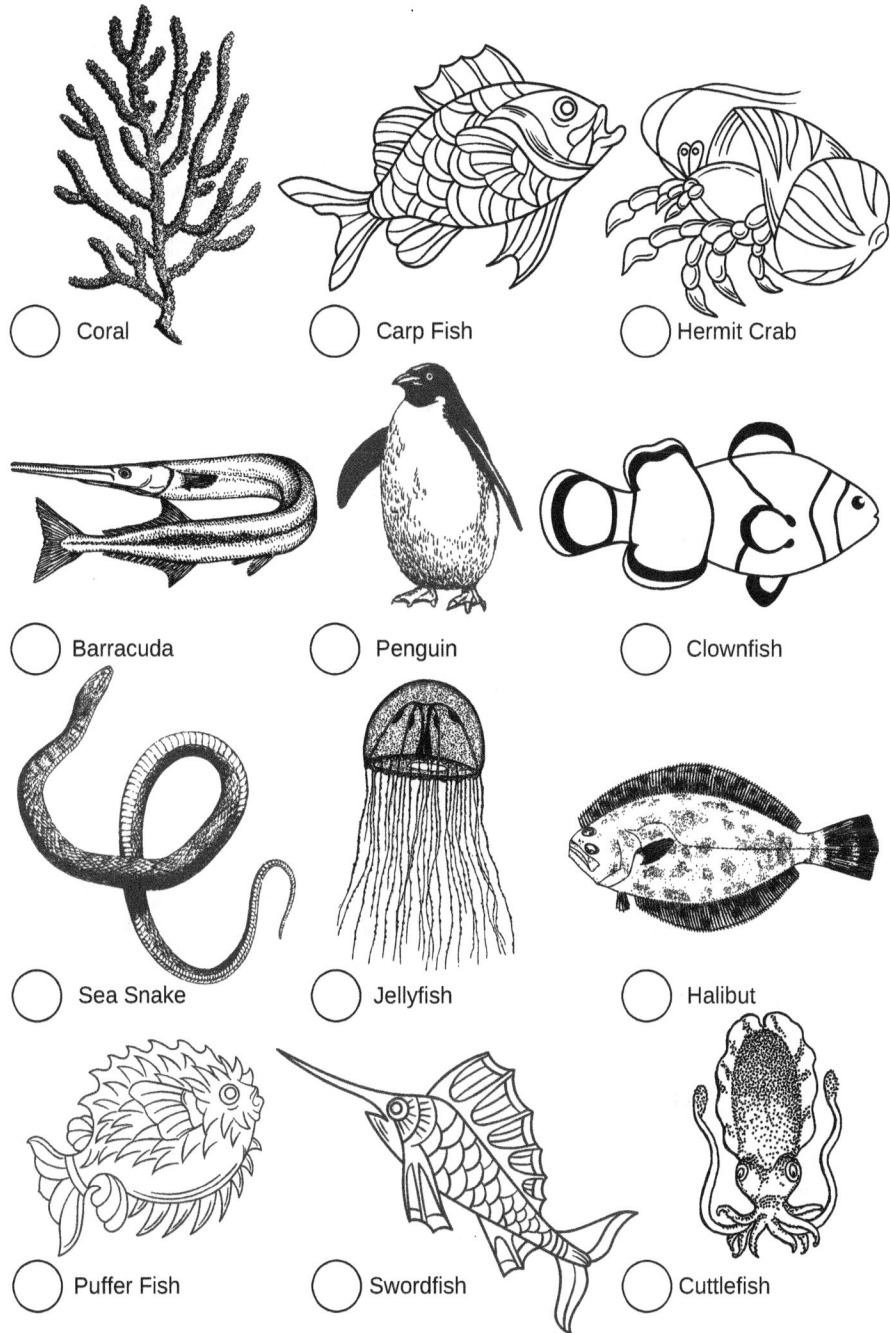

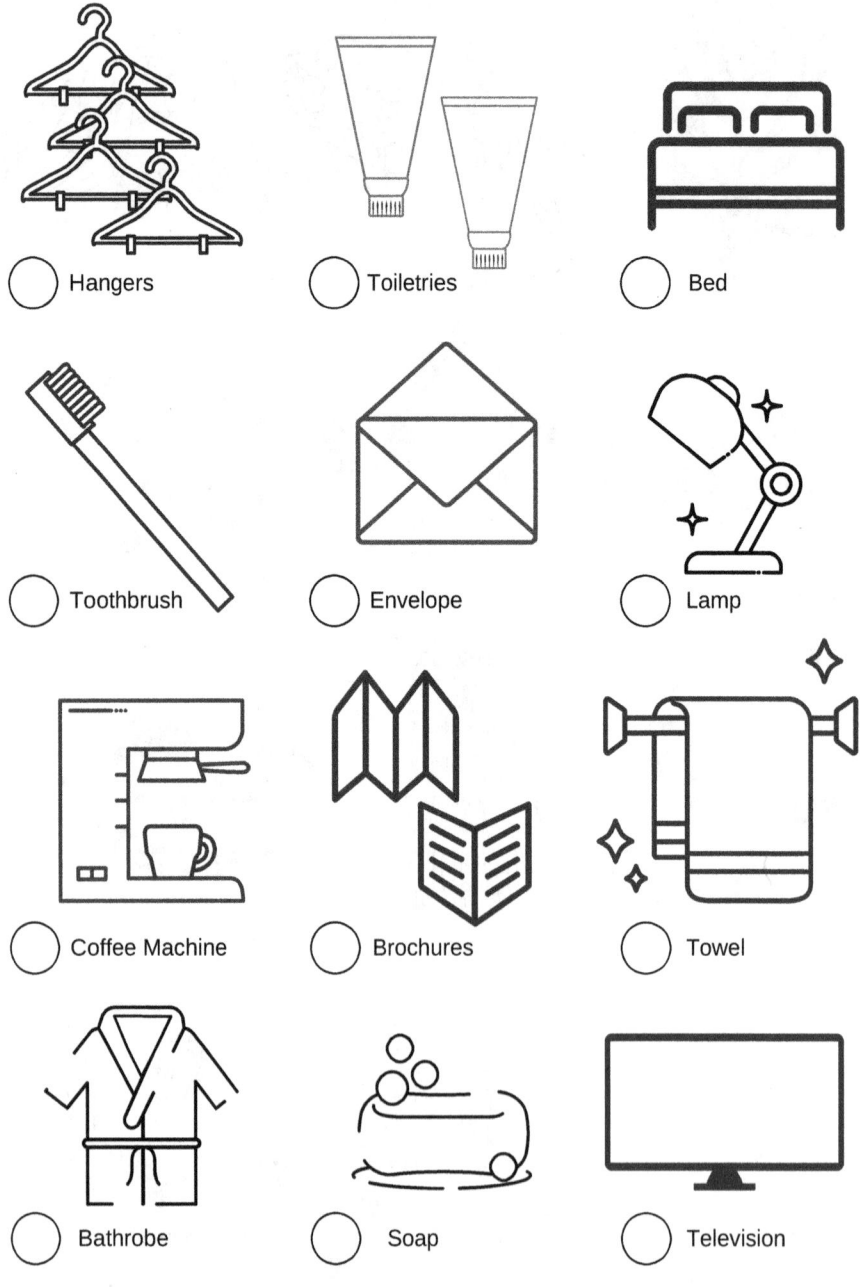

MY HOTEL LIST

- ◯ Local Map
- ◯ Pen
- ◯ Plant
- ◯ Four Chairs
- ◯ Clock
- ◯ Two Bottles of Water
- ◯ Desk
- ◯ Fire Extinguisher
- ◯ Cartoons on the TV
- ◯ Exit Sign
- ◯ Room Number Sign
- ◯ Curtains

MY FALL LIST

MY FALL LIST

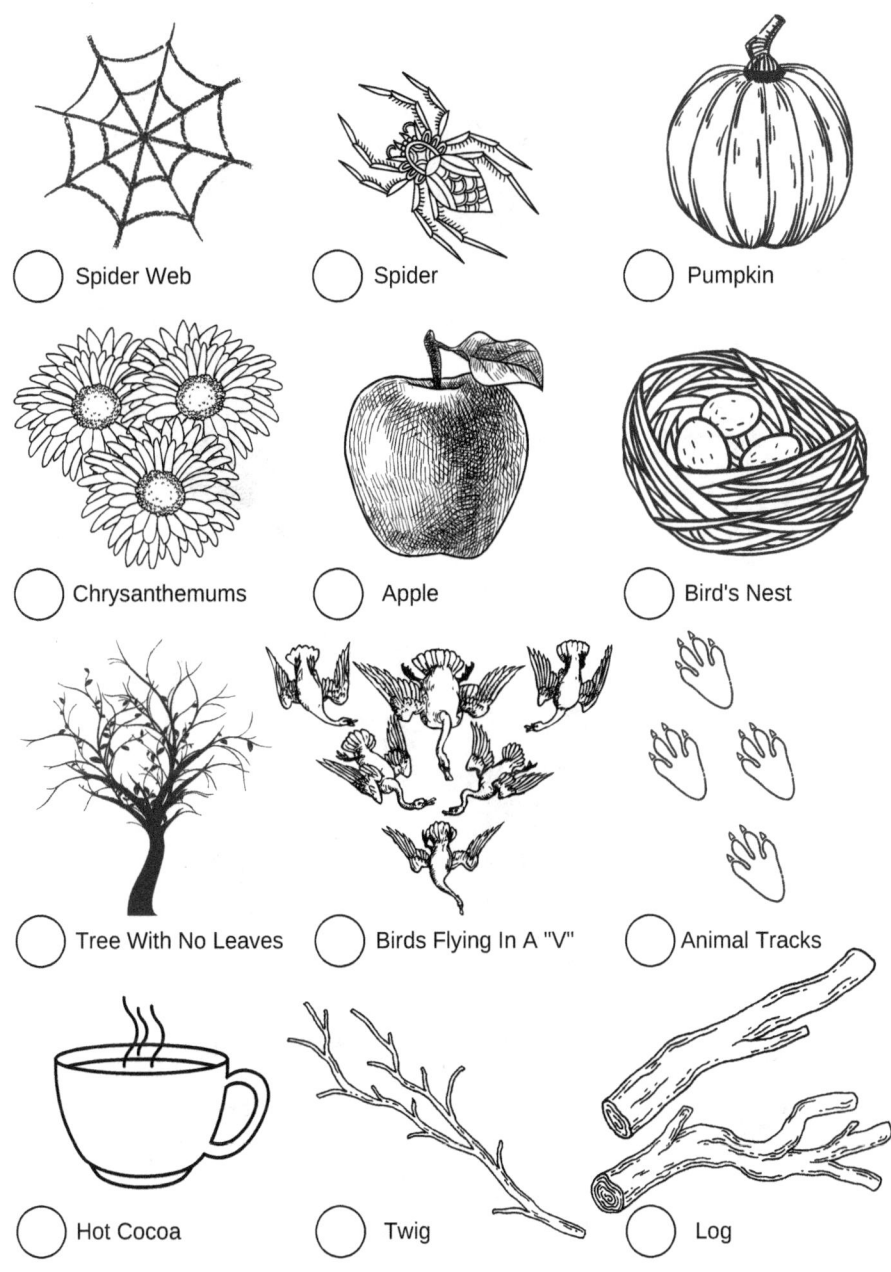

MY WINTER LIST

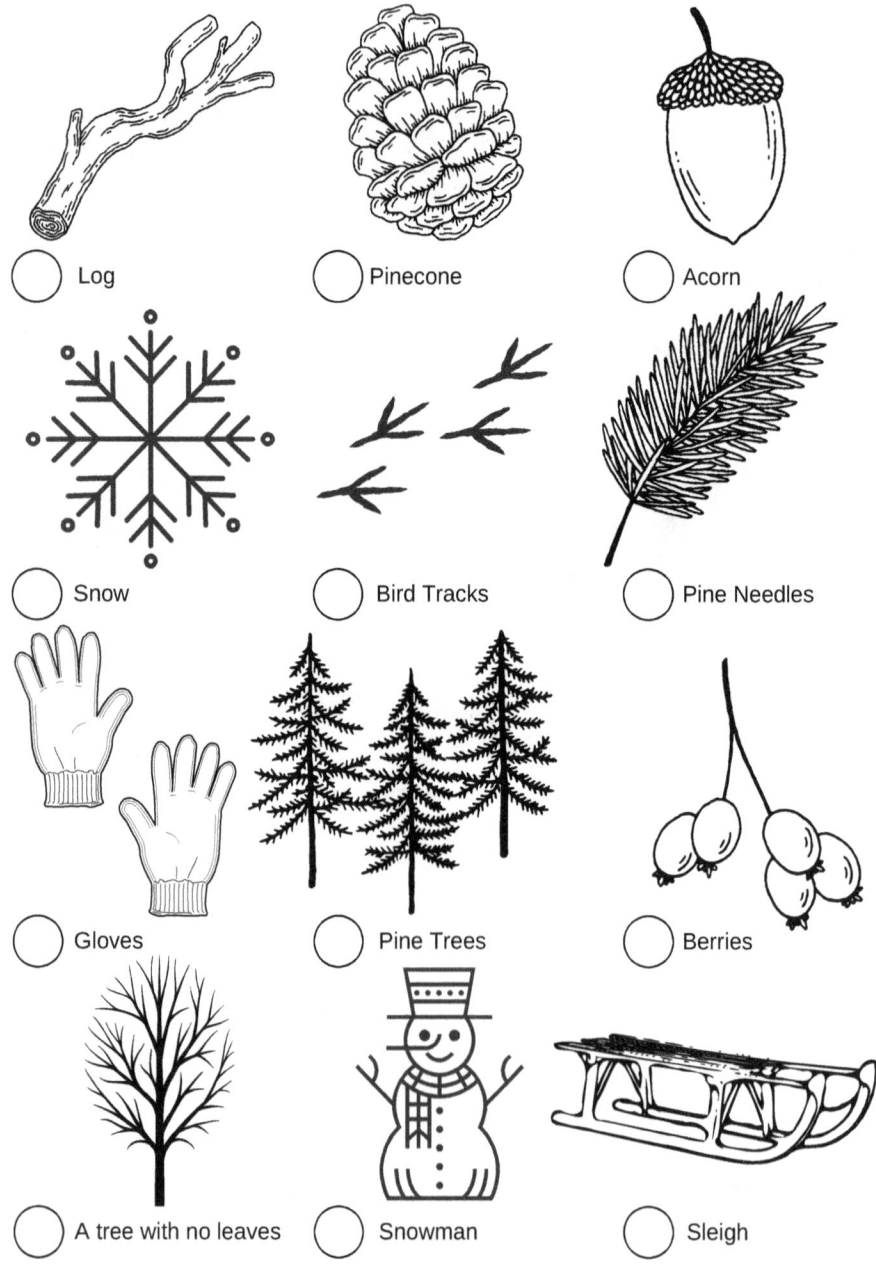

MY WINTER LIST

- Warm Hat
- Bird
- Exhale Cloud
- Toad
- Dead Leaves
- Squirrel
- Cookies and Milk
- Hot Chocolate
- Animal Tracks
- Scarf
- Ice Skates
- Sweater

MY SPRING LIST

MY SPRING LIST

○ Dandelion ○ Grasshopper ○ Strawberries

○ Ducklings ○ Umbrella ○ Feather

○ Squirrel ○ Rain ○ Ant

○ Sunshine ○ Puddle ○ Seeds

MY SUMMER LIST

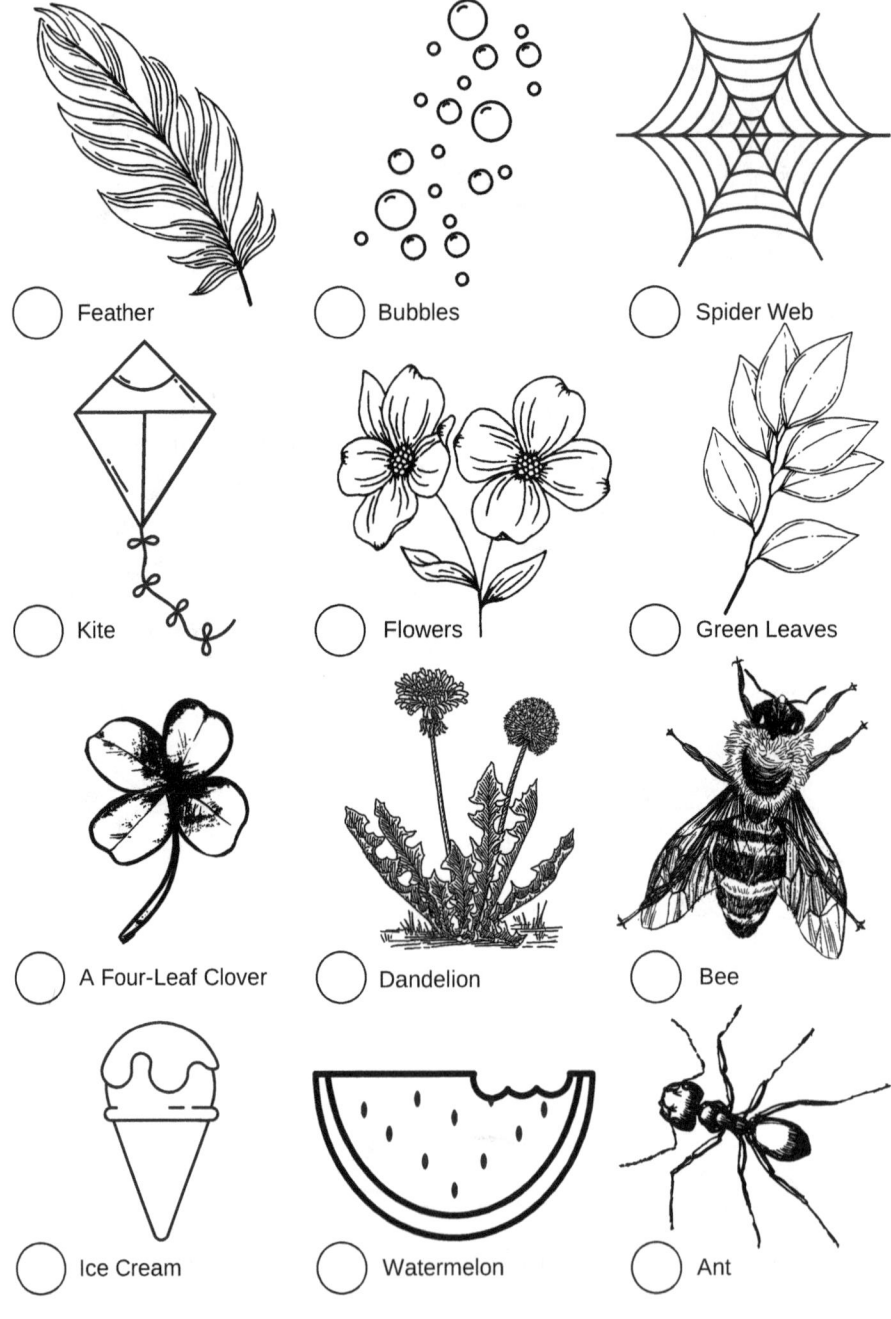

MY SUMMER LIST

- ◯ Sunglasses
- ◯ Beach Ball
- ◯ Butterfly
- ◯ Ice Cubes
- ◯ Swimsuit
- ◯ Flip Flops
- ◯ Sun
- ◯ Tie Dye Shirt
- ◯ Sunscreen
- ◯ Tent
- ◯ Lemonade
- ◯ Dragonfly

MY MARKET LIST

MY MARKET LIST

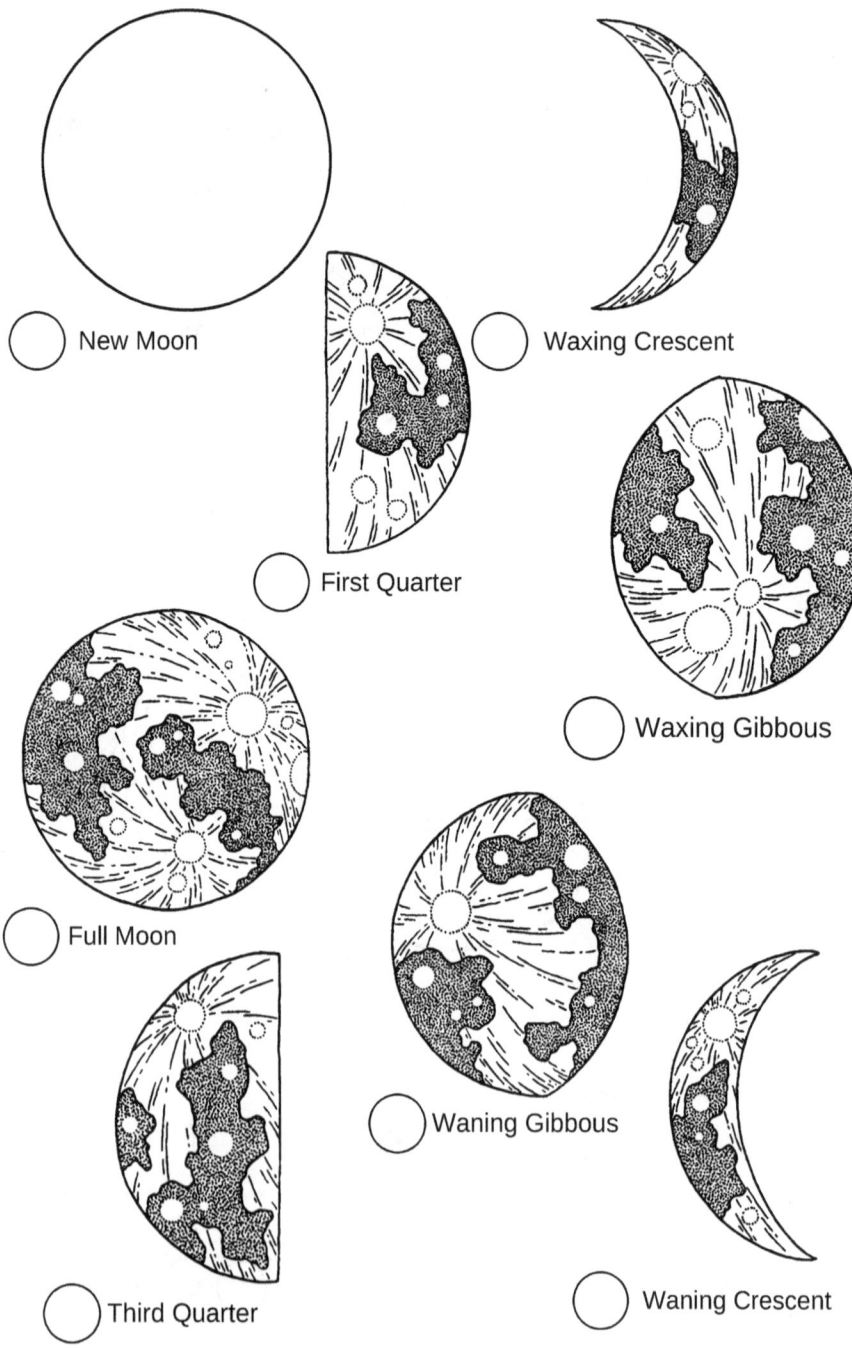

MY SHAPE LIST

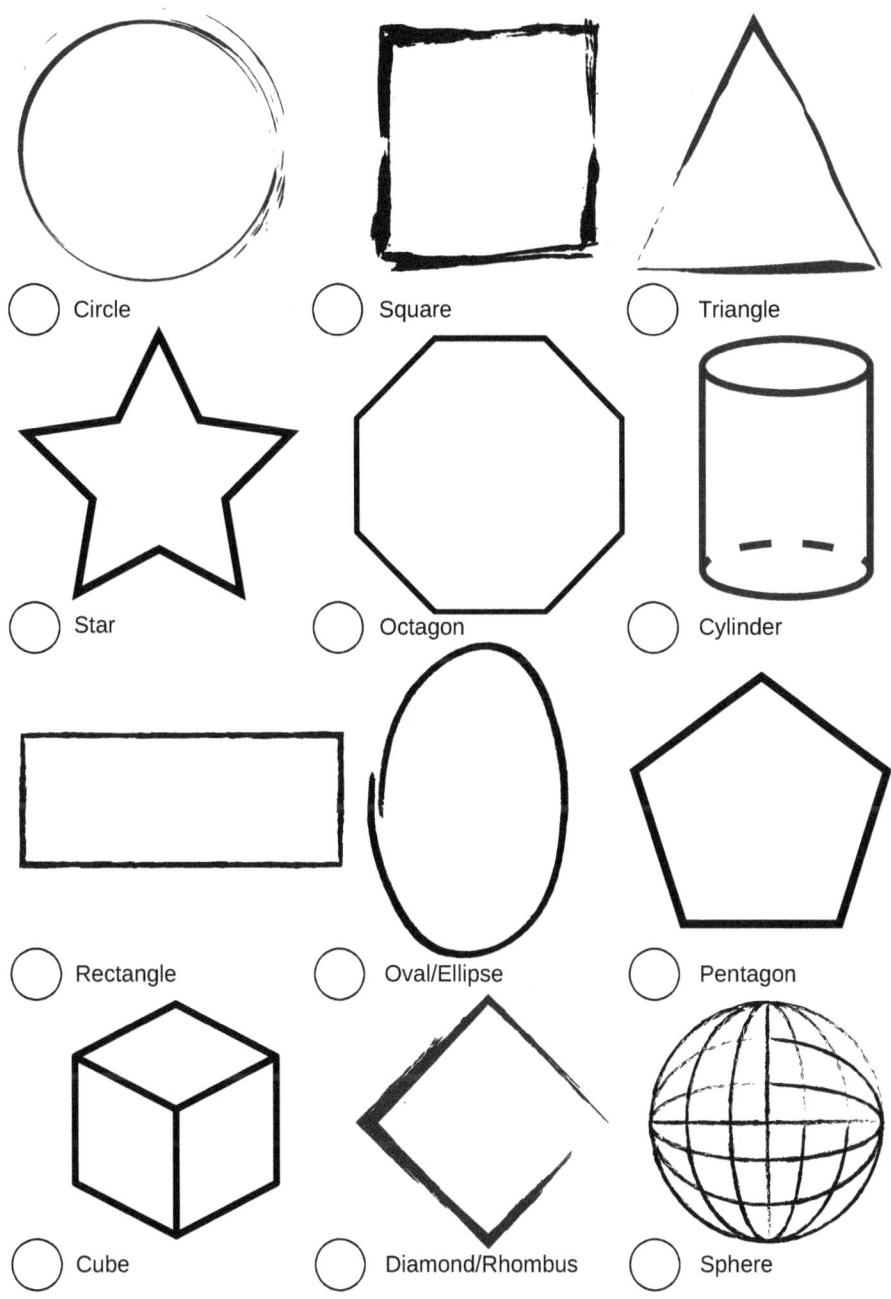

MY SEASIDE LIST

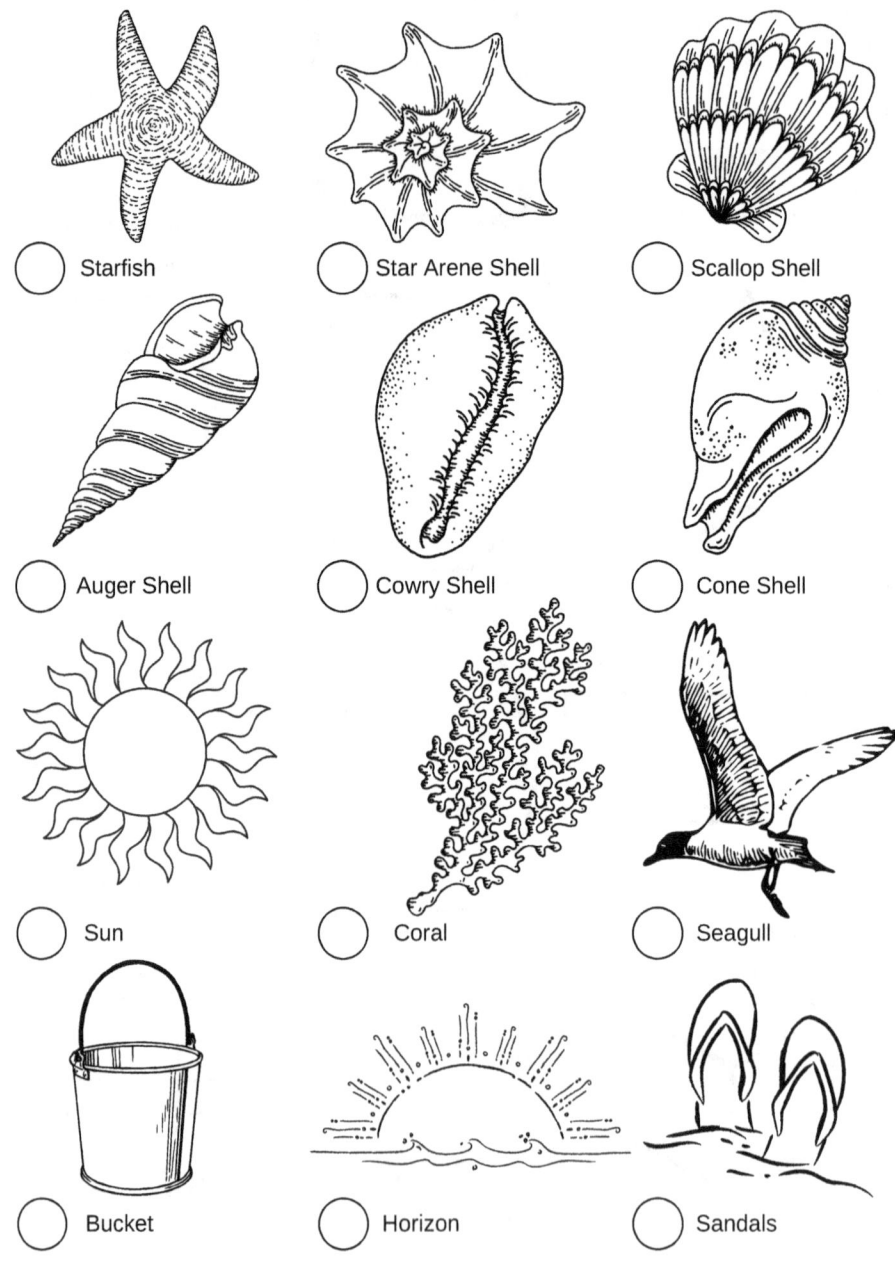

MY SEASIDE LIST

○ Sand Castle
○ Shovel
○ Seaweed
○ Beach Sign
○ Sunglasses
○ Crab
○ Sunscreen
○ Salty Breeze
○ Kite
○ Boat
○ 5 Pieces of Litter (Pick It Up to Throw Away)
○ Water Bottle

MY FOREST LIST

MY FOREST LIST

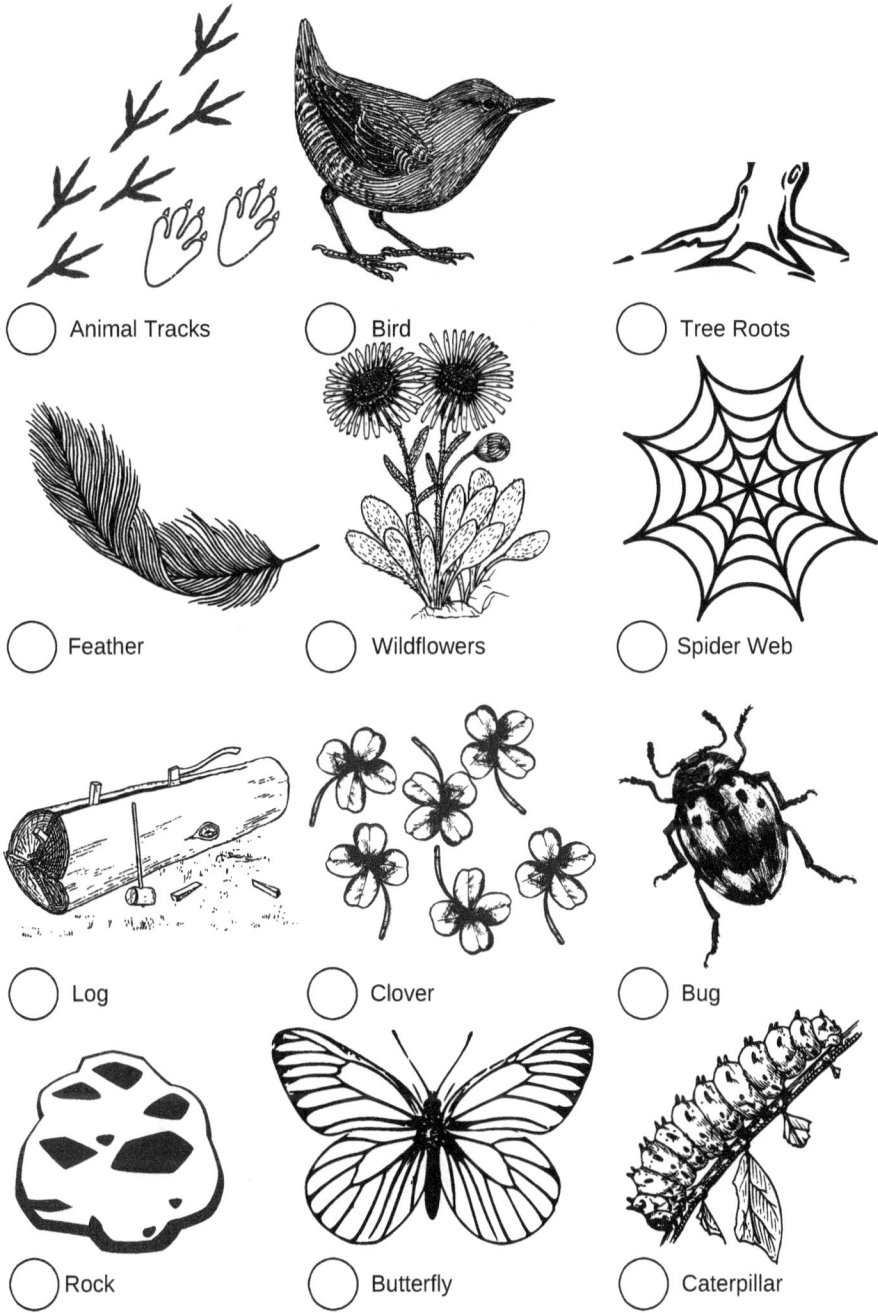

MY ART CLASS LIST

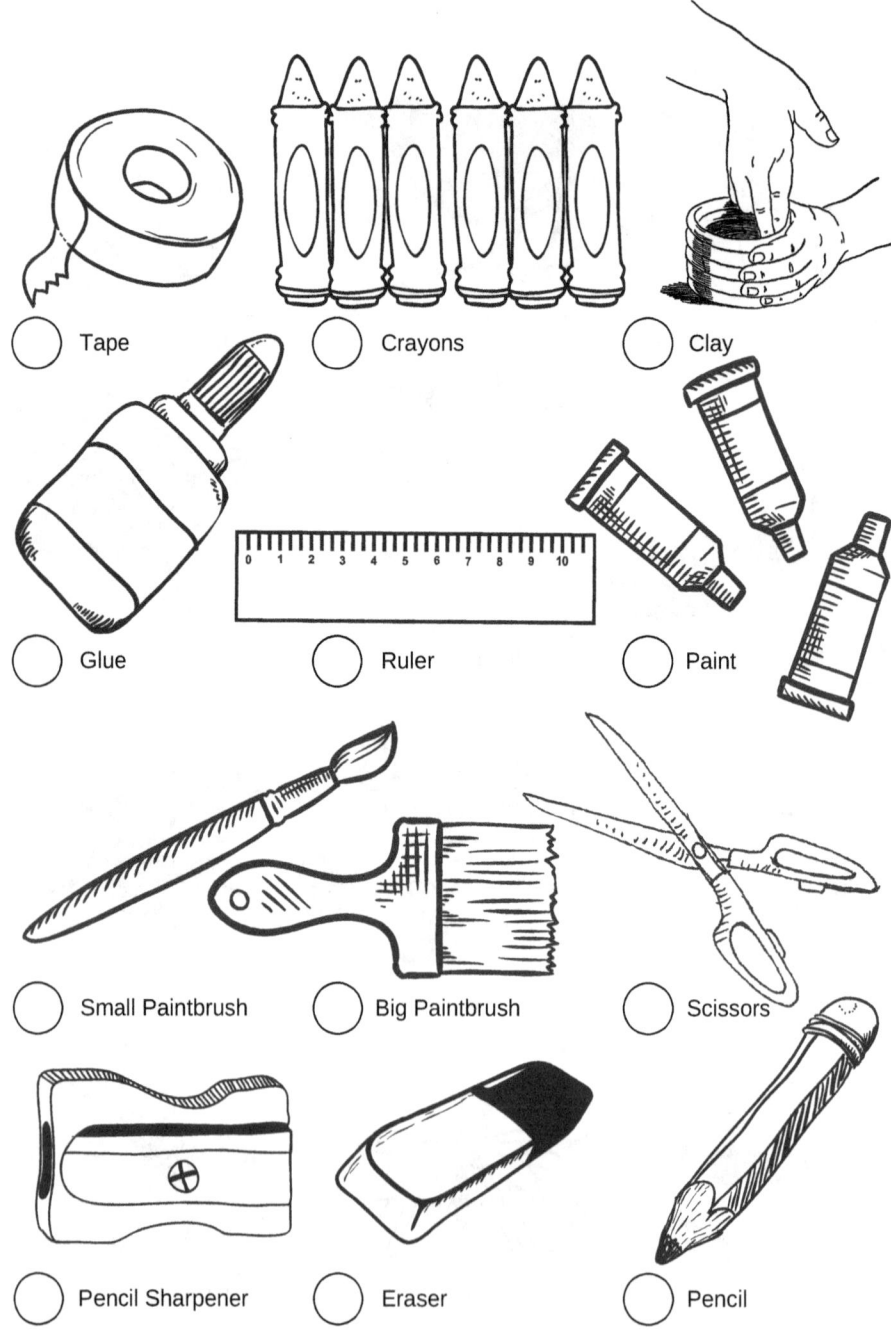

- Tape
- Crayons
- Clay
- Glue
- Ruler
- Paint
- Small Paintbrush
- Big Paintbrush
- Scissors
- Pencil Sharpener
- Eraser
- Pencil

MY MUSICAL INSTRUMENT LIST

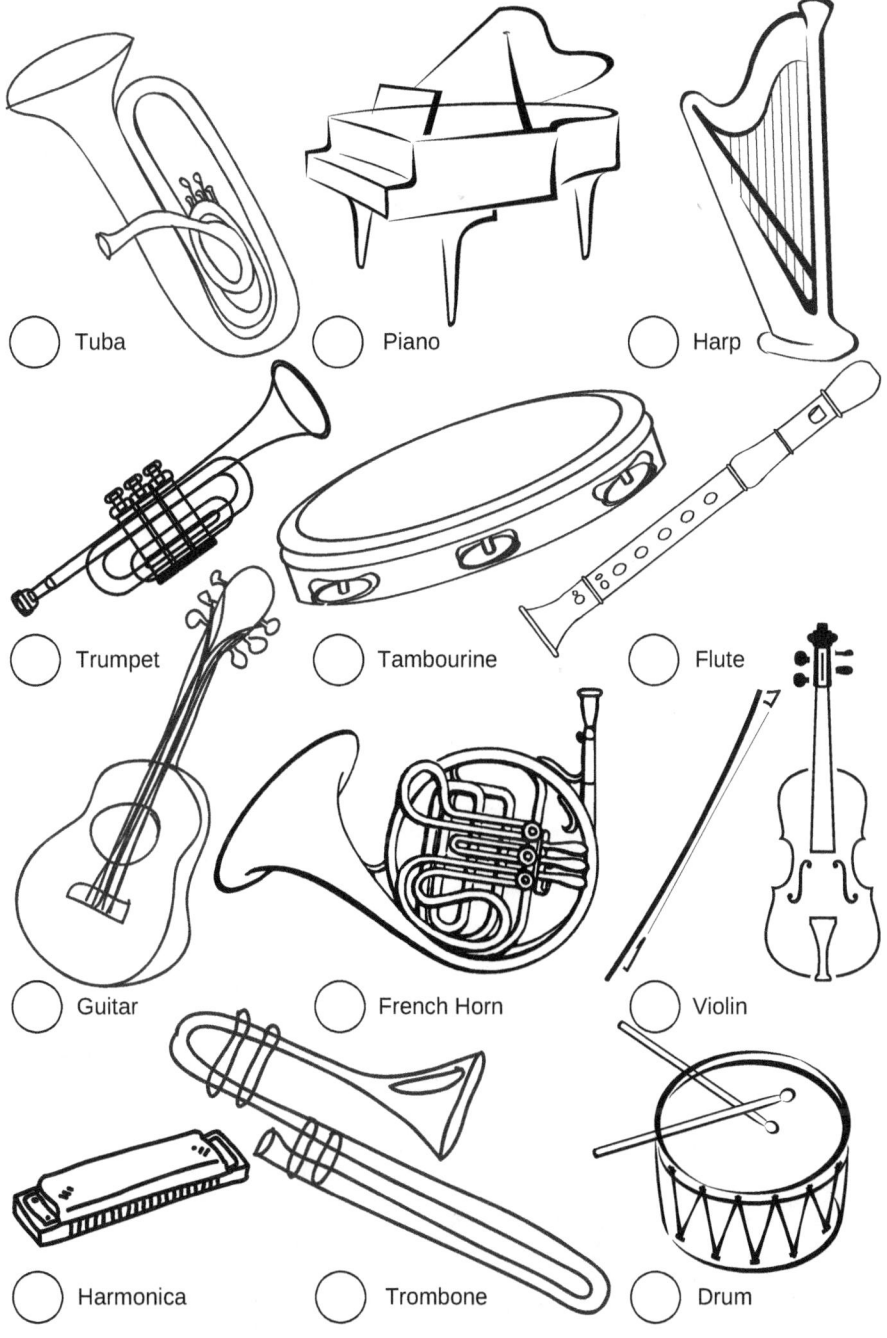

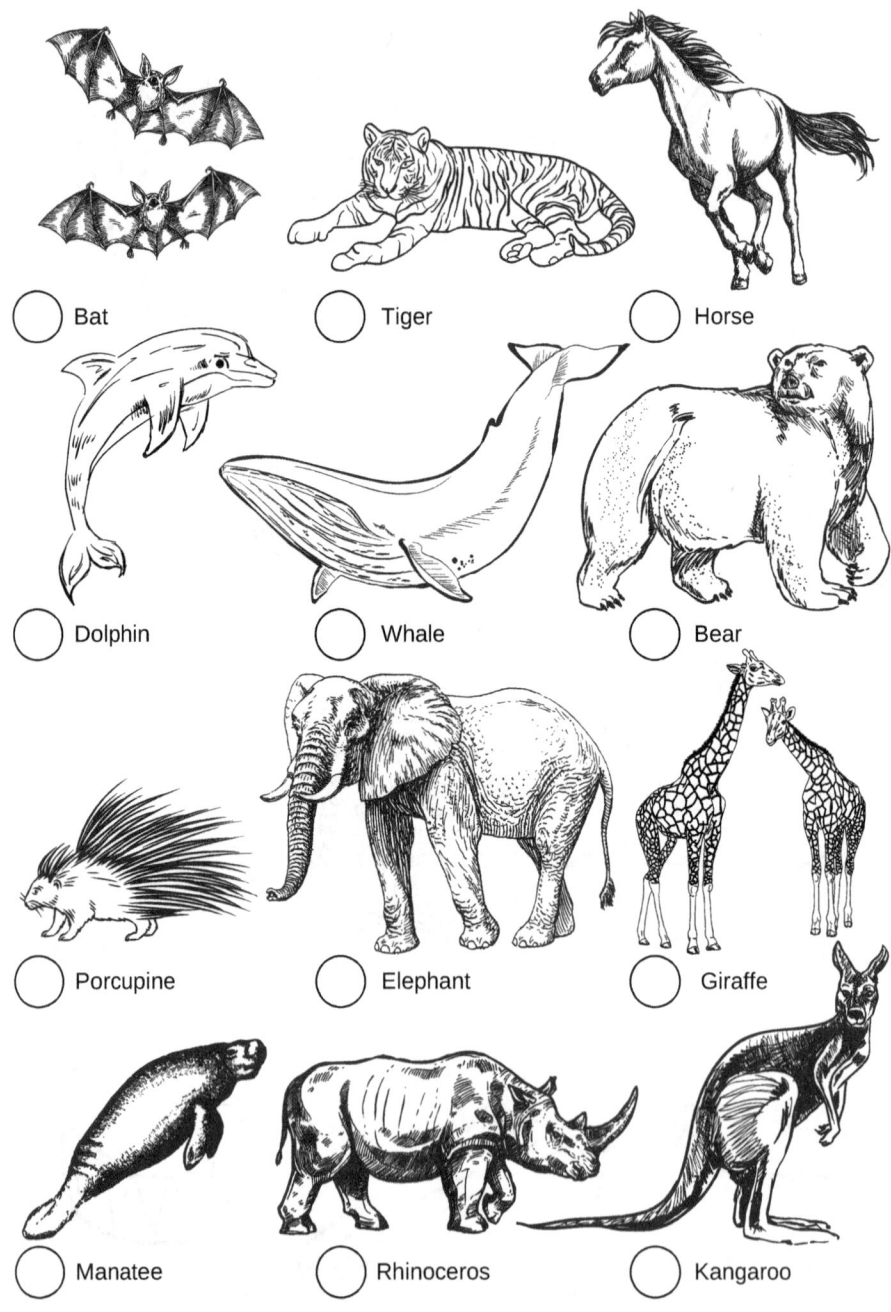

MY BIRD LIST

◯ Eagle ◯ Penguin ◯ Hummingbird
◯ Pelican ◯ Duck ◯ Ostrich
◯ Macaw ◯ Owl ◯ Chicken
◯ Heron ◯ Seagull ◯ Peacock

MY REPTILE & AMPHIBIAN LIST

○ Chameleon   ○ Rattlesnake   ○ Tree Frog

○ Mudpuppy   ○ Iguana   ○ Salamander

○ Alligator   ○ Skink   ○ Turtle

○ Horned Frog   ○ Komodo Dragon   ○ Gecko

MY FISH LIST

- ○ Catfish
- ○ Clown Fish
- ○ Snapper
- ○ Swordfish
- ○ Tuna
- ○ Piranha
- ○ Bluegill
- ○ Angelfish
- ○ Salmon
- ○ Halibut
- ○ Guppy Fish
- ○ Koi Fish

MY DINOSAUR LIST

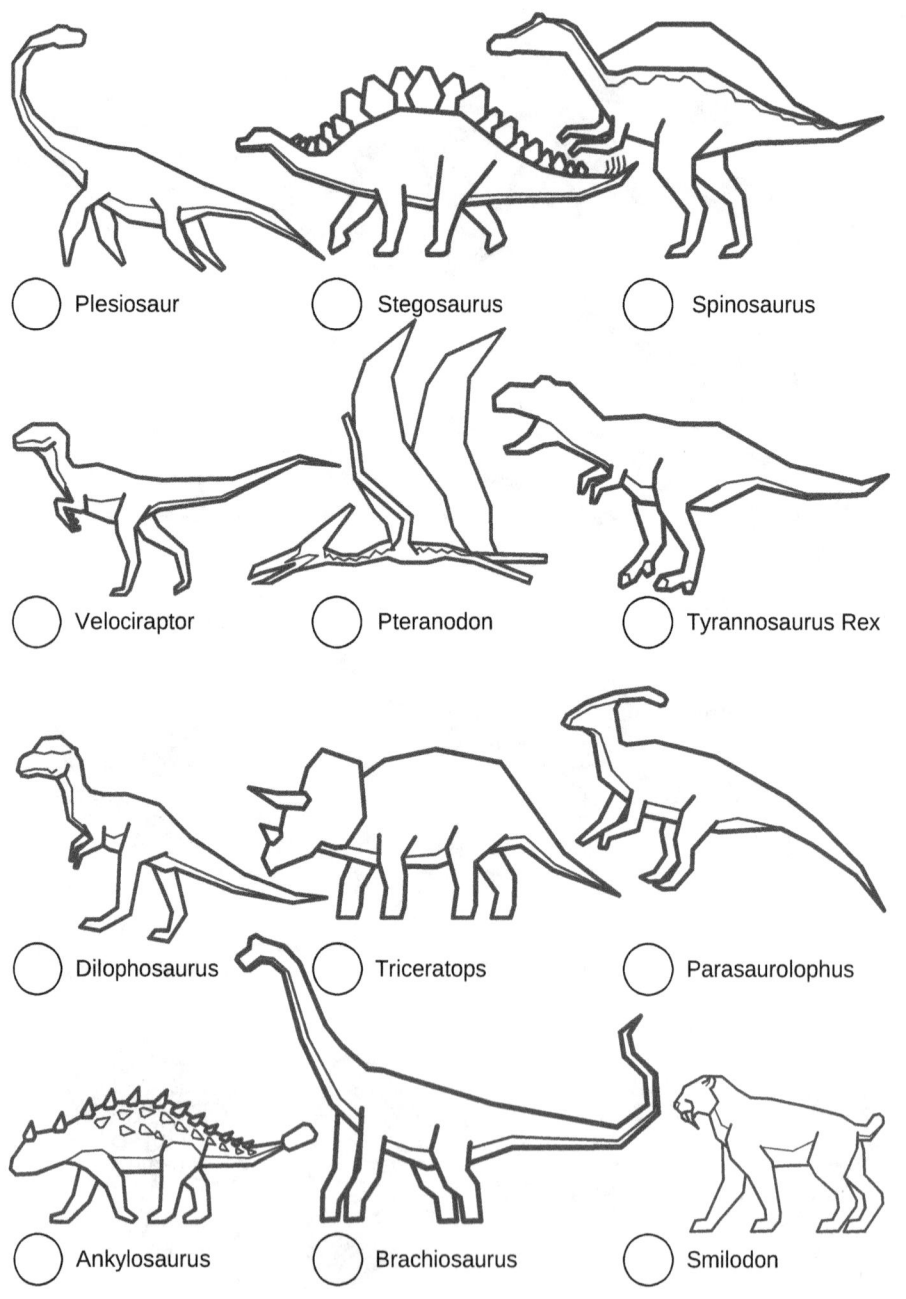

○ Plesiosaur ○ Stegosaurus ○ Spinosaurus

○ Velociraptor ○ Pteranodon ○ Tyrannosaurus Rex

○ Dilophosaurus ○ Triceratops ○ Parasaurolophus

○ Ankylosaurus ○ Brachiosaurus ○ Smilodon

www.ingramcontent.com/pod-product-compliance
Lightning Source LLC
Chambersburg PA
CBHW061348040426
42444CB00011B/3136